NATIONAL
GEOGRAPHIC

Celebrate FAMILY

PIONEER EDITION

By Patricia McKissack and Elizabeth Sengel

CONTENTS

Family

By Patricia McKissack

Ties

What makes you who you are? Study your family's past. You may find some answers. Be a detective. Find the clues to your family tree.

Look in the mirror. Do you see your grandma's eyes? Do you see your dad's smile? That's no surprise. We get our looks from our family.

Families give us much, much more. They hand down favorite foods and traditions. They also share stories. Where did your mother's grandmothers live? What were they like? These stories make you and your family special.

History Detective

Do you want to learn about your family? Genealogy can help you. It's the study of people who are related to you. They may be people you know or people who lived long ago.

Genealogists are like detectives. They look for clues in public records. Some records tell when and where people are born. Others tell about marriages and deaths. Some even tell when people first came to the U.S. Newspapers, letters, and those old family stories may hold clues, too.

3

Smiling Faces. *These photos show special times in Carson's life. Pictures like these help to trace family histories.*

Ancestor Names

In the 1800s and 1900s, millions of people came to America. They arrived at Ellis Island in New York. Professor Henry Louis Gates, Jr., visited there. He wanted to learn about his African American ancestors. Yet he didn't find any records at Ellis Island.

You see, the first African Americans did not go to Ellis Island. Most came on ships full of enslaved people. Then they were sold to owners. The owners split families. They gave people new names. Family histories were lost.

Still, Gates found family stories of nine African Americans. One was the story of his friend Ben Carson's family. Carson is a famous brain doctor.

Beginnings

Ben Carson grew up poor. His mother, Sonya Copeland, worked three jobs. Family members took care of Carson while his mom worked.

At first, Carson didn't do well in school. But his mother pushed him to do better. She would not let him fail.

Carson admired his mother's strong will. He wanted to know about her past. Professor Gates helped him.

Gates listened to family stories. He looked through old pictures, public records, and papers. Gates traced Carson's family to white owners. They lived in Georgia in the 1800s. Their last name was Copeland, just like Carson's mother!

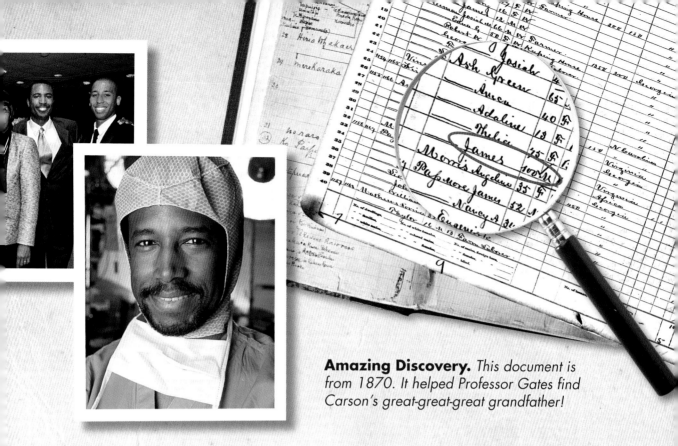

Amazing Discovery. *This document is from 1870. It helped Professor Gates find Carson's great-great-great grandfather!*

Strong Spirit

William Copeland, Sr., was a white owner. When he died in 1859, his family sold his things. Gates found a **document** that showed what happened to a child named John H. Copeland. He was Carson's great-grandfather.

John was sold and sent away from his family. What became of him? Amazingly, Gates found John's name in the 1870 census. That's a count of everyone who lives in the U.S.

John's name was listed on the census with his mother's. Somehow, the child had found his way back to his family! Maybe this is where the determination of Carson's mother came from.

Back to Africa

The 1870 census had another big surprise. It listed a 100-year-old man named James Ash. The census said he was born in Africa. Gates figured out that Ash could be Carson's ancestor!

It is rare to find proof that a person sold into enslavement came from Africa. Gates found this great clue on paper. Next, he turned to science.

In the Lab

Gates knows DNA holds our body's **genes**. They are instructions that control how we look. Genes are passed down in families. So they can tell where our ancestors came from. Gates ran DNA tests. They showed some of Carson's ancestors came from Cameroon, Nigeria, and Kenya.

Your Turn!

Carson was glad to learn about his past. You can learn about your past, too. First, ask your family questions—lots of questions! Who were your grandparents' parents? Where did they live? What were they like?

While you listen, take notes. Write down all the names, places, and dates you hear. Use audiotape or video to record stories. Then you can listen to the stories again later.

Research

You can use what you learn to make a family tree. Draw a tree like the one below. Write your name at the top. Then write the names of your relatives. It's OK if you don't know all the names.

Now you can be a detective! Go to a library. Search for family names in old newspapers. Look on the Internet. Keep a folder of family letters and photographs. They could be clues, too.

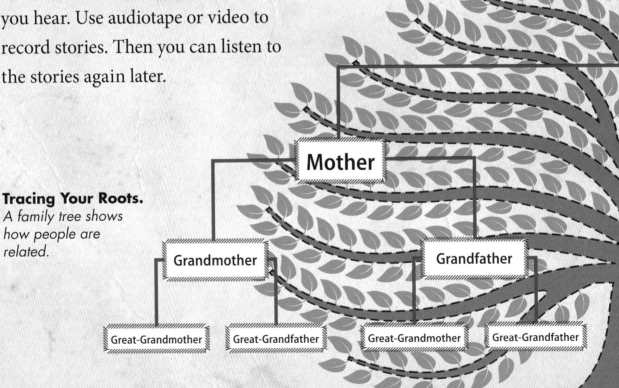

Tracing Your Roots.
A family tree shows how people are related.

Mother

Grandmother — Grandfather

Great-Grandmother | Great-Grandfather | Great-Grandmother | Great-Grandfather

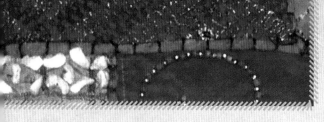

Share Stories

You can also make a family memory book. Make a page for each person. Then ask each relative to write a personal story. Add family photos, newspaper clippings, and drawings to each page.

At your next family party, pass the memory book around. Ask family members to add more memories. Just think of the new stories you might hear!

Celebrate

Telling stories keeps your family history alive. Trade tales about your Great-Grandpa Max and your Grandma Sylvia.

Write a family newsletter. You can take turns writing stories. That way everyone gets to help.

You may know you have your grandma's eyes. Maybe you have your dad's smile. Now you know a lot more about your family!

Wordwise

document: paper that gives information

gene: something inside the body that parents pass down to children and that controls how the children look

genealogist: person who studies family history

ou

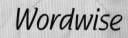

Father

Grandmother

Grandfather

Great-Grandmother Great-Grandfather Great-Grandmother Great-Grandfather

A Nation of Names

THIS MAP SHOWS POPULAR last names in different parts of the United States. The captions and the key tell where the names came from.

How did researchers make the map? They looked in phone books to find the top last names in each state. Then they used computers to figure out where the names came from.

The name Smith came from England. It is the most popular last name in the United States. Can you find your name?

Many names near Mexico came from Spain.

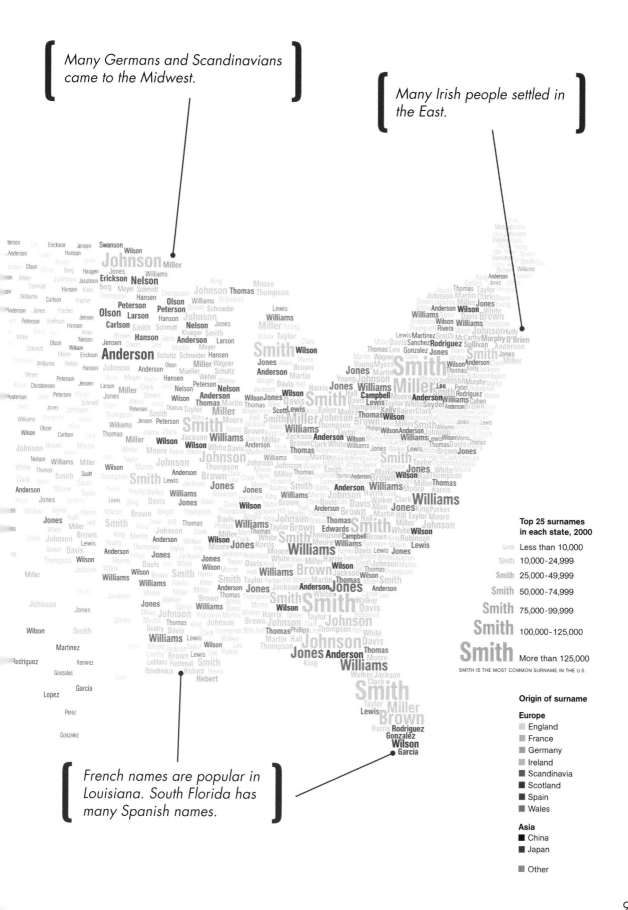

Many Germans and Scandinavians came to the Midwest.

Many Irish people settled in the East.

French names are popular in Louisiana. South Florida has many Spanish names.

Top 25 surnames
in each state, 2000

Smith Less than 10,000
Smith 10,000-24,999
Smith 25,000-49,999
Smith 50,000-74,999
Smith 75,000-99,999
Smith 100,000-125,000
Smith More than 125,000
SMITH IS THE MOST COMMON SURNAME IN THE U.S.

Origin of surname

Europe
England
France
Germany
Ireland
Scandinavia
Scotland
Spain
Wales

Asia
China
Japan

Other

A Wealth of

When people come to America, they bring more than their names. They bring traditions, too. Here are some traditions from other places. They help make life in America richer.

Dragon Dance. *A dragon is part of a New Year parade in San Francisco.*

Summer Celebration. *Children in Kansas dance to celebrate summer.*

Lee: CHINESE

New Year is important for many Chinese people. Family and friends get together. They welcome the new year.

People sweep out the old year. They clean their houses from top to bottom. They whisk away the past.

Chinese Americans celebrate New Year in January or February. One of the biggest events is a dragon parade.

During the parade, a long dragon dances down city streets. Firecrackers whiz and pop. The firecrackers keep the dragon awake for the celebration!

Anderson: SCANDINAVIAN

In countries like Sweden and Denmark, warm summer days are very popular. In those places, winter days are short. So people love summer!

Scandinavian people celebrate summer at a midsummer festival. It takes place in late June. That's when the days are at their longest.

Scandinavian Americans carry on this custom. People dress in colorful costumes. Women wear flowers in their hair. Children hold hands and sing as they dance.

Traditions

By Elizabeth Sengel

Smith: AFRICAN AMERICAN

Many African Americans took a new name, such as Smith, when they came to America. They may not have kept their names. But they kept their traditions.

Take quilts, for example. African Americans used big shapes and strong colors for quilts. This was a custom that came from Africa. There, people made fabric with big designs and bright colors. The cloth helped people see one another from far away.

African Americans made quilts to keep warm. They made them to tell stories. And they made quilts to help remember family members.

Memory Quilts. *This is an African American story quilt. It is in a museum in Boston.*

Garcia: MEXICAN

The strum of guitars. The sweet sound of violins. The blare of trumpets. What is that sound? Mariachi!

Mariachi music began in the 1800s. It started in the Mexican state of Jalisco. Today, it is popular around the United States. Mexican Americans—and many other fans— join bands to play mariachi music. The bands perform at concerts and festivals around the country.

Mariachi musicians wear wide-brimmed hats. They wear fancy suits and boots. They sing songs about love and other emotions.

Mariachi Melodies. *Mariachi musicians play violins in Texas.*

Focus on
FAMILY

Family traditions are important. Answer these questions to celebrate them.

1 How is the study of family history like detective work?

2 What did Professor Gates do to research Dr. Ben Carson's family history?

3 What events happened in the life of John H. Copeland, Ben Carson's great-grandfather? List them in order.

4 Choose one of the family traditions from the article. How does it celebrate family history?

5 Why are family histories, names, and traditions important?